I Love Sports
Cheerleading

by Kaitlyn Duling

Bullfrog
Books

Ideas for Parents and Teachers

Bullfrog Books let children practice reading informational text at the earliest reading levels. Repetition, familiar words, and photo labels support early readers.

Before Reading

- Discuss the cover photo. What does it tell them?

- Look at the picture glossary together. Read and discuss the words.

Read the Book

- "Walk" through the book and look at the photos. Let the child ask questions. Point out the photo labels.

- Read the book to the child, or have him or her read independently.

After Reading

- Prompt the child to think more. Ask: Have you ever seen cheerleaders in action? What was your favorite part?

Bullfrog Books are published by Jump!
5357 Penn Avenue South
Minneapolis, MN 55419
www.jumplibrary.com

Library of Congress Cataloging-in-Publication Data

Names: Duling, Kaitlyn, author.
Title: Cheerleading / by Kaitlyn Duling.
Description: Minneapolis, Minnesota: Jump!, Inc., 2018. | Series: I love sports | Includes index.
Audience: Age 5–8. | Audience: K to Grade 3
Identifiers: LCCN 2017022345 (print)
LCCN 2017019264 (ebook) | ISBN 9781624966682 (ebook) | ISBN 9781620318201 (hardcover: alk. paper)
Subjects: LCSH: Cheerleading—Juvenile literature.
Classification: LCC LB3635 (print)
LCC LB3635 .D85 2018 (ebook) | DDC 791.6/4—dc23
LC record available at https://lccn.loc.gov/2017022345

Editors: Jenna Trnka & Jenny Fretland VanVoorst
Book Designer: Leah Sanders
Photo Researcher: Leah Sanders

Photo Credits: IPGGutenbergUKLtd/iStock, cover, 20–21, 23bl; BCFC/iStock, 1; cmannphoto/iStock, 3; Image Source/Getty, 4; stevecoleimages/iStock, 5; ViewApart/iStock, 6–7, 23tr; huronphoto/iStock, 8; william87/iStock, 9; Lopolo/Shutterstock, 10–11; LSOphoto/iStock, 12–13, 23mr; Doug Pensinger/iStock, 14, 23br; monkeybusinessimages/iStock, 15; Ivica Drusany/Shutterstock, 16–17, 23tl; William Perugini/Shutterstock, 18–19, 23ml; Lokibaho/iStock, 22; Duplass/Shutterstock, 24.

Printed in the United States of America at Corporate Graphics in North Mankato, Minnesota.

Table of Contents

Let's Cheer!

Tie your shoes.

Grab your friends.

Let's cheer!

Today is the big game.
The squad gets ready.

Mia loves to yell.
Her voice is loud!

8

Sam does jumps.
She points her toes.

9

Time for a stunt.

Ann is a base.

She is strong.

She holds the flyer.

flyer

base

11

They make a pyramid.

Wow!

Cam tumbles.
He runs.
He flips.

The crowd loves it!

Here is the mascot.

He is silly.

He has spirit.

pom-
pom

Sara smiles wide.
She dances.
She uses pom-poms.

Do you have spirit?

You can cheer.

Go team!

Time for a Stunt!

flyer
The person on the top of a stunt. The flyer is lifted into the air.

spotter
Someone who offers support to bases and flyers during a stunt.

base
One of the people at the bottom of a stunt. The base lifts the flyer.

pyramid
Stunt in which two or more people support a tier of higher people, who in turn may support other, higher tiers of people.

Picture Glossary

mascot
A person who wears a costume and gets the crowd excited.

squad
A group of people who cheer together.

pom-poms
Brightly colored handheld fluffy balls used by cheerleaders.

stunt
A performance in which participants lift each other into formations.

spirit
Enthusiasm.

tumbles
Performs acrobatics, such as flips and cartwheels.

Index

To Learn More

Learning more is as easy as 1, 2, 3.

1) Go to www.factsurfer.com

2) Enter "cheerleading" into the search box.

3) Click the "Surf" button to see a list of websites.

With factsurfer.com, finding more information is just a click away.